THE UNR[illegible]Y: UNITY WI[illegible]GELICALS

In the discussion an[illegible] controversy which followed the publication of Evangelicalism Divided: A Record of Crucial Change in the Years 1950–2000[1], *the author was invited by Dr John F. MacArthur to give an address on the book's main theme. The following is the substance of that address, given at the Shepherds' Conference on 11 March 2001.*

All books have a story of some kind behind them. They come into existence and take their shape in many different ways. It may help to introduce the subject before us if I begin by saying something on the origin of *Evangelicalism Divided*. In Britain the year 1996 marked the thirtieth anniversary of an event which became a milestone in the evangelical history of our country. Thirty years before, on 18 October 1966, Dr Martyn Lloyd-Jones spoke at a National Assembly of Evangelicals in London. His subject was *Evangelical Unity*. At the end of his address the chairman, the Rev. John R.W. Stott, instead of closing the meeting, did something unscheduled. He took several minutes to make clear to the assembly that he disagreed with

[1] Edinburgh: Banner of Truth, 2000. References for all quotations given here will be found in the book itself.

what they had just heard, and he gave some reasons. So a conference intended to promote evangelical unity had the opposite result. It was said that evangelical unity was fractured; some said it was 'wrecked'. Who was to blame for that outcome? On the anniversary of that event, thirty years later, the question was again being discussed, both in magazines and in books. It figured prominently, for instance, in the biography of Dr James I. Packer, published in 1997. My interest in this renewed debate prompted me to give an address on the subject in Australia in February 1998.

At that date, while I was still in Australia, I came across the sympathetic and definitive biography of Billy Graham, *A Prophet With Honor*, written by William Martin. One might suppose that a biography by an American and on an American would have no connection with the difference which had occurred among British evangelicals, but the Graham biography provides strong confirmation that there was indeed a connection. As the Martin book further opened out the subject for me, it became clear that the disagreement in London in October 1996 had to be understood in a much wider context, for to a surprising degree the main issue was the same on both sides of the Atlantic. This led me to research the subject more thoroughly, and in the course of two years my initial address grew into the recent book.

There are personal reasons why I found the theme difficult to handle. For one thing, *Evangelicalism Divided* is a sad book. I found it sad to think about and sad to write. One reason for this is that the subject has to do with a difference, not between the good and the bad, but between genuine, eminent, Christian men. The devil has often used the strategy of distracting believers from their work by provoking them into controversy with each other. In that way, instead of strength being united against a common enemy, energies are weakened and opportunities are lost. The Book of Genesis pointedly tells us that at the time when the unhappy strife between Abram's servants and those of his nephew Lot occurred, 'the Canaanite and the Perizzite dwelled then in the land' (*Gen.* 13:7). Scripture means us to note the words and to be warned. Our first duty is to love one another, not contend with one other. When disagreement among Christians cannot be avoided, it should be a cause of pain, and we ought to do all we can not to aggravate it. The wisdom which is from above, says James, is 'peaceable', and I have tried to write with respect and esteem for evangelicals with whom I have to disagree. But, lest any should find *Evangelicalism Divided* depressing, I need to add something which is really obvious. The book, of course, is not intended in any sense to be a history of the gospel in the last fifty years. In that period there have been great spiritual blessings across the world and my theme is in no sense a denial of that reality.

A further difficulty for me in writing the book was this: As the subject developed I was not able to record events merely as an onlooker. Rather I found myself confronted with a searching, humbling question. As I thought that other evangelicals made mistakes and erred in judgments, I was forced to ask myself how I might have fared had I been in their situations, and subjected to the same pressures as they faced. Unusual success, popularity, and eminent positions are dangerous things. For those of us who have little exposure to such dangers, it is easy to imagine how much better we might have done. But the reality is that we could have done worse than those with whom we differ. We share a common frailty and proneness to err. We are all 'unprofitable servants'. 'We all stumble in many things', says James (3:2). The more I saw this, the more I found my whole subject to be a humbling one. Sometimes we may have to disagree with other believers, and even to disagree strongly, but at the same time it is imperative that we watch ourselves and our own motives. We are fellow-servants in Christ and Paul's words are very searching:

> But why do you judge your brother? Or why do you show contempt for your brother? For we shall all stand before the judgment seat of Christ . . . So then each of us shall give account of himself to God' (*Rom*.14: 10, 12).

I come then to the main question before us: When we talk about evangelicalism divided, what was the cause of the division to which we are referring? What were Lloyd-Jones and John Stott disagreeing about? To ask this question leads us immediately into the controversy because, strange as it may sound, to this day there is no agreement over what the difference actually was! This much is clear: It was not over any basic evangelical belief. No fundamental truth was being denied or opposed by either side. Both sides held to Scripture and to the Person and work of Christ. How then could there be such a serious difference? To explain I need to give you a brief résumé of some British history.

Liberalism, Evangelicals and the Ecumenical Movement

It is agreed that the use of the term 'evangelical' is simply another way of describing a person or a denomination that believes the gospel. In the middle of the nineteenth century, all Protestant denominations in the country were evangelical in their statements of belief. But then a great decline began. Liberalism entered our pulpits, and it came in the name of Christ. It spoke much of devotion to Jesus. It used traditional Christian language. Christ, it said, is to be experienced, admired and followed. A crucial difference between its message and historic Christianity, let me remind you, was over how anyone enters into real Christian experience. Liberalism taught that faith comes from our own human intuition; all that is needed is a well-disposed heart.

It held that there can be faith in Christ without revealed truth and an authoritative Bible. People can have genuine experience of Christ quite apart from doctrinal beliefs. 'Christianity is life not doctrine', was the great cry. The promise was that Christianity would advance wonderfully if it was no longer shackled by insistence on doctrines and orthodox beliefs.

That kind of teaching swept through the British denominations, and it instituted a new definition of a Christian. An unbeliever in the fall of man, or the atonement, or the deity of Christ, could now be said to be a Christian. This thinking had innumerable representatives. A professor of theology in Edinburgh, who died in 1960, affirmed that a person could be a 'believer' without knowing it. It is possible, he said, for individuals to deny God with the 'top of their minds' yet believe in the bottom of their hearts. In that same year, 1960, a leading British politician died and, despite his atheism and indifference to Christianity, he was honoured in Westminster Abbey, the main shrine of the national Church. Archbishop Michael Ramsey – to whom I will refer more fully later – defended that action with the words, 'Heaven is not a place for Christians only . . . I expect to see some present-day atheists there.'

True gospel believers – that is, evangelicals – were dismayed at what they saw happening in the churches after the rise of liberalism in the nineteenth century. Two courses were open to them. Some left the mainline denominations. C. H. Spurgeon, the most notable example, left the Baptist Union in 1888. Others stayed within and, because they were too few to exercise any discipline, they lived largely apart from the non-evangelicals of their own denomination who generally were in the positions of leadership. Further, these evangelicals, whether still in the main denominations or outside them, kept up a regular association among themselves by means of a common membership in various non-denominational organizations. In these agencies, biblical beliefs were preserved and non-evangelicals were excluded. So Evangelicalism was a unity transcending denominations; in a number of respects it approximated to Fundamentalism in the States, and American fundamentalists were welcomed by evangelicals in the United Kingdom. A characteristic of an evangelical was that he put his evangelical commitment before denominational allegiance and, while he was happy to work in evangelism and conventions with evangelicals of other denominations, he avoided corporate witness and activity with those who were not of like faith. Evangelical organizations, such as the Inter-Varsity Fellowship, had Statements of Faith which were definitely intended to prevent the membership of liberals.

When Billy Graham came to Britain, on his first major crusade at Harringay, London, in 1954 he was welcomed by evangelicals. But he was not welcomed by the denominational leaders. No denomination had agreed to sponsor his crusade. Archbishop Ramsey equated Evangelicalism with Fundamentalism and called them both 'heresy'. Of Graham he said, 'He has taught the grossest doctrines and flung his formula "the Bible says" over teaching which is emphatically not that of the Bible.'[1] But then a remarkable thing happened. As the crusade went on through three months, with many thousands attending, religious leaders and the religious press began to show interest and by the time it ended liberals who had stood far apart at the beginning were even to be found sitting on the evangelist's platform. At the final meeting no less a person than the Archbishop of Canterbury, Dr Fisher, gave the benediction.

Why this change of attitude among those who had not been known for belief in conversion and gospel preaching? That question is crucial to an understanding of what was to follow. A number of evangelicals, especially those in the Church of England, made up their minds that they knew the answer. They were persuaded that something very

[1] *British Weekly*, 9 February 1956. Ramsey's verdict at the end of the Crusade was, 'He has gone. Our English fundamentalism remains. It is heretical.'

important was happening; they spoke of witnessing 'the beginning of another Evangelical Revival' – a movement which could change the face of the churches. They believed they were seeing something which they had never seen before, and perhaps had never expected to see, namely, preachers who denied the substitutionary atonement and the fall of man sitting quietly under such preaching and apparently approving the evangelist. Surely this was evidence that a non-evangelical ministry was recognizing the emptiness of its message and was looking for something better.

This was one explanation of the apparent change of attitude among non-evangelicals, and those who accepted it began to think that some change would also be appropriate on their part. Not a change of belief but a re-think of the policy of standing apart from liberals. Perhaps if evangelicals were more willing to co-operate with those of other views they might win them, just as Graham appeared to be doing. Perhaps it was their own fault that they had enjoyed small influence, compared with the 38,000 decisions registered at Harringay.

Just at this point in time another powerful influence was at work, in all the mainline denominations and across the English-speaking world. The ecumenical movement was in its ascendancy and promising that a new era of Christian influence was at hand if only all Christians would unite. Ecumenism stood for a new openness, with charity for all opinions. One result of this charity was that, instead of being cold-shouldered, evangelicals now had the new experience of being invited to play a full part in their denominations and in the wider unity movement. If they accepted this opportunity they were assured of an influence which had previously escaped them. They had been living 'in a ghetto', it was said; let them come out and they would be welcome to take their share in places of leadership.

It was while ecumenism was speaking in this way that, simultaneously on both sides of the Atlantic, a new evangelical policy was being born. It began in the States before it took hold in England. Its main advocates were Fuller Seminary, *Christianity Today,* and the Billy Graham Evangelistic Association, and for a time these three new institutions became something of a threefold cord which could not be broken. The same leaders stood related to all three. Together they shared the common conviction that Fundamentalism had been too separatist, too negative, too exclusive. Evangelicals needed to make their voices heard in the mainline denominations. Many Christians were still to be found there and, with a wise approach, the denominations might yet be won back to the faith. The policy, for a time called the 'New Evangelicalism', was to concentrate on the positive, especially on evangelism, on better scholarship. It sought to take advantage of the ecumenical ethos to gain a new respect for Scripture.

Many things happened which appeared to demonstrate the success of this policy, and the co-operation of non-evangelicals in the Graham crusades seemed to endorse its correctness. No less a figure than Archbishop Michael Ramsey himself became a supporter. In 1961, Dr Graham accepted an invitation to the Conference of the World Council of Churches in New Delhi. There he met the man who had described his beliefs as heresy in 1956, and in his autobiography Graham records this portion of the conversation which took place between them:

> Dr Ramsey, could we – you and I – be good personal friends? Do we have to part company because we disagree in methods and theology? Isn't that the purpose of the ecumenical movement, to bring together people of opposing views?

The response, as Graham tells us, was this: 'A strong supporter of the ecumenical movement, he had to smile and agree with my logic.' Thereafter the two men were to be friends.

It was this same policy which now came to be advanced in England, especially by evangelicals in the Church of England. John Stott, one of the the youngest of these men, is said to have acted as the unofficial chaplain to the Graham team during the Harringay Crusade. He now became the leader among the younger generation of Anglican evangelicals, and their new policy was summarized in the words, 'Co-operation without Compromise'. The outworking of this policy led, in 1967, to the first National Evangelical Anglican Congress, and the guest invited to speak at the opening of the Congress was Michael Ramsey. The Archbishop used the occasion to tell his hearers that 'experience goes before theology', that they must learn from each other, and if the evangelicals were prepared to play a full part in the life of the Church of England, they must turn their backs on their old exclusiveness. When it was all over, the published Congress statement included these words, in a section on 'Dialogue': 'The initial task for divided Christians is dialogue, at all levels and across all barriers.

We desire to enter this ecumenical dialogue fully. We are no longer content to stand apart from those with whom we disagree.' This exciting Congress was spoken of as part of a new evangelical renaissance. A corner had been turned and the old isolationalism – as it was now called – was to be a thing of the past.

To summarize, I repeat that this new-look evangelicalism was not new with respect to beliefs. It stood and intended to stand for biblical Christianity. It was new rather in policy and strategy, and in my book I do not argue that this was wholly mistaken. The older Evangelicalism and Fundamentalism is not to be defended on all points. Some change was needed. Without question, a number of the influences which came out of the alliance of Fuller Seminary, *Christianity Today* and the Billy Graham Evangelistic Association were good. And many souls were brought to real faith in Christ under Graham's ministry. All that is to be remembered with thankfulness. Where then lay the problem? What caused the division among evangelicals?

Two Principal Explanations

1. The new emphasis on 'openness', and on the wider co-operation of evangelicals with others, failed to address the fundamental problem in the mainline denominations. That problem was the way in which the definition of a Christian had been changed and undermined. A different idea of what it meant to be a Christian was very widespread, both in pulpits and in pews. Scripture teaches that faith in the gospel of Christ is indispensable for salvation; liberalism believes that men and women can have 'the Christian life'

without the Christian faith. Charles Hodge states the divergence in these words:

> A man who believes certain doctrines is a Christian. If his faith is mere assent, he is a speculative Christian; if it is cordial and appreciating, he is a true Christian. But to say that a man may be a Christian, without believing the doctrines of Christianity, is a contradiction. A man may be amiable and benevolent, without any definite form of faith, but how is he to be a Christian?

Contrary to those words, the starting point of the ecumenical movement is that all who say they are Christians, on a minimum profession of faith, are to be accepted as such. It saw no reason to question that assumption. So the priority for the churches, according to ecumenism, is not a recovery of the faith and of truths essential to salvation, it is the uniting of those who say they are already believers. In a day when liberalism was dominant in almost all the main denominations, the ecumenical church leaders were ignoring the main problem. The possibility that teachers and people had adopted the Christian name without ever meeting with the risen Jesus did not seem to come into their reckoning.

In this situation, evangelicals had a crucial problem. If agreeing to the ground rule, 'We are all Christians', was necessary to gain ecumenical and denominational acceptance, how could such agreement be consistent with the uniqueness of their beliefs? If evangelical belief is, in essence, gospel belief, how can Christian fellowship exist independently of any common commitment to that belief?

And how can a right belief on fundamentals retain the primary importance which Scripture gives to it if, after all, that belief is not necessary to salvation? Or to put the same question another way, How can evangelicalism be said to represent biblical essentials if one regards as Christians and works alongside those who actually deny these essentials?

This was the point which Lloyd-Jones took up in his address at the meeting of October 1966 which brought on the disruption. His central point was that, as fellowship and brotherhood in Christ depend on gospel belief, the unity with which evangelicals should be concerned has to be evangelical not ecumenical. 'We should be asking: What is a Christian? How do we get forgiveness of sins? And, What is a church?' He believed that for evangelicals to appear to accept the 'We are all Christians' axiom of ecumenism was fundamentally wrong.

The Lloyd-Jones message cut right across the policy which was becoming popular in evangelical circles. In response to him it was said that the issue was really only about churchmanship, and that Lloyd-Jones was simply repeating the old separatist message which led men into backwaters and minimal influence. No, he replied, the issue was the practice of evangelical belief. The faith can be undermined in practice, he warned, even where it is held in principle. Very few evangelical leaders thought the warning was relevant. One who did was Francis Schaeffer. In the same year as the Lloyd-Jones address in London, Schaeffer spoke at the Berlin Congress on Evangelism, where he said:

> Let us never forget that we who stand in the historic stream of Christianity really believe that false doctrine, at those crucial

> points where false doctrine is heresy, is not a small thing. If we do not make clear by word and practice our position for truth as truth and against false doctrine, we are building a wall between the next generation and the gospel.

In other words, if the practice of broad co-operation did not stop, the distinctiveness of the gospel would be lost. A difference of conviction over this point was a main cause of division.

2. Another explanation of the division has to do with difference of opinion over the depth and reality of human depravity. I do not mean that one side denied human sinfulness, but it is possible to have a correct definition of the fall of man and yet act in a way that fails to take sufficient account of Christ's commandments, 'Beware of men' (*Matt.* 10:17); 'Beware of false prophets which come to you in sheep's clothing' (*Matt.* 7:15). The teaching of Scripture on the deceitfulness of the human heart is given to us for urgent practical reasons. 'Take heed to yourselves', and 'Watch', are constant biblical injunctions (*Acts* 20:28-31; *1 Tim.* 4:16, etc).

I believe the success of the early Graham crusades, and the new evangelical policy, was connected with a failure to give sufficient weight to the warnings of Scripture on human nature. Both in the States and in Britain, the support of non-evangelicals and even of open liberals came to be deliberately sought in crusade evangelism. I have given you one explanation why this change of attitude occurred among evangelicals. The willingness of non-evangelicals to co-operate was interpreted as heralding a significant change of spirit; it was believed that one-time opponents of evangelical belief were becoming its friends. So the caution which previously characterized the relationship of evangelicals with others was now replaced with openness and optimism.

But there is another interpretation of the change on the part of liberals and I am afraid it is the true one. This is not merely my opinion for, these many years later, we have the biographies and writings of a number of the church leaders who were one-time crusade supporters. In repeated instances they reveal that there was no change in their beliefs at all. They were simply impressed with the numbers attending Graham's ministry and were interested in channelling some of the crowd into their own churches. Men such as Dr Leslie Weatherhead and Archbishop Ramsey said as much. 'What does fundamentalist theology matter,' Weatherhead said to fellow-liberals, 'compared with gathering in the people we have all missed.' In the 1966 London crusade Archbishop Ramsey told his clergy to receive those referred to them 'whatever one thinks of the theology'.

Ramsey's biography gives us this illuminating anecdote. By coincidence the Archbishop had planned to be in Rio de Janeiro, Brazil, in 1974 at the same time that a Graham crusade was being held in the city. When Graham heard this news, he at once invited Ramsey to come and speak for a little at the opening meeting. Ramsey's biographer writes that he 'did not believe in crusades'; nevertheless he accepted the invitation and Graham wrote to him to say he was 'overwhelmed with gratitude . . . we come from such diverse religious backgrounds and yet . . . this glorious unity.' Before the meeting the Archbishop went over the notes of what he intended to say with the Portuguese-speaking interpreter. The man, a Brazilian Presbyterian pastor, objected that 'he could not translate all that on grounds of conscience'. In this impasse, the issue was taken to Graham who insisted that the Archbishop was his guest and that the translator must interpret every word. So among other things, the audience that night heard these words from the Englishman:

> You cannot come to Christ unless you bring your Roman Catholic brother with you . . . If you are asked to come forward to testify to Christ, don't come unless you bring with you a resolve to be more charitable to your Roman Catholic brothers.

This was extraordinary news for Brazilian Christians who had left the Church of Rome, where they had known nothing of brotherhood in Christ.

Sometimes, no doubt, liberals were converted under Graham's ministry, but it is not being cynical to say that the widespread interest of non-evangelicals in his crusades was commonly related to advancing their own agenda. They were using him, as an official of the World Council of Churches admitted when he said, 'We do not agree with Billy Graham's theology, but we are using him to build our churches.' I need hardly remind you how Graham defended what he called his 'ecumenical strategy'. What did it matter, he said, who co-operated and who associated with the crusades, provided the preaching stayed in evangelical hands. But the truth was that he wanted the co-operation of these men for the aid that their reputations gave to his work, and for the way it could secure wider denominational support. Winning the mainline denominations remained the primary objective, and that could not be done without the good will of the leaders. So both sides were motivated by an ulterior motive. On Graham's side the motive was to get a wider hearing for the gospel, but in order to do this he adopted an attitude towards false teachers which is not compatible with the New Testament.

The new evangelicalism on both sides of the Atlantic was so hopeful of success that such words as, 'Beware of men', seemed to be out of place and uncharitable. Men who had never preached the gospel in their lives now came to be regarded as basically good. 'Billy won't believe anything bad about a person', said his associate, Robert Ferm. Even in his autobiography, Dr Graham appears to be unconscious of the way he was repeatedly used by men for their own ends. He describes, for instance an afternoon in the White House with President Clinton in these terms:

> It was a time of warm fellowship with a man who has not always won the approval of his fellow Christians but who has in his heart a desire to serve God and do his will.

This is not an isolated example of naivety in the realm of the political. After another lapse on his part Graham was heard to say, 'I was like a babe in the woods, I didn't know what was going on.' Such failure becomes the more dangerous when it involves assessment of preachers and the spiritual. To me the saddest words in the whole of Martin's long biography of the evangelist occur in the following quotation which he includes:

> Those who know Billy best say that it is his amiable personality that makes him believe he can become a sort of pontiff – or bridge-builder – between Bible-believing Christians and those attractive personalities who are the proponents of the non-redemptive gospel. [At a recent breakfast] he pleaded with us to recognize that many liberals were good men, loved the Lord, and perhaps could be won over to the conservative position . . . Billy spreads himself too thin; he tries not to offend anybody in any way . . . Not making war on some things he has gone to the other extreme, and made peace, not with the doctrines of apostasy, but with those who preach the doctrines of apostasy. This, I believe, is deadly and will one day defeat the whole cause for which this man of God is labouring.

The Evangelical Change and Its Results

I offer these two points as explanation of the cause of division. As I have already mentioned, from the other side a different explanation is put forward for the evangelical disunity in Britain. After 1966 Lloyd-Jones began to break off public co-operation with the evangelicals who were committed to promoting unity with non-evangelicals. For this he was greatly blamed. Evangelicals on the other side, such as John Stott and Jim Packer, recommended a double commitment: They wanted to continue a commitment to fellow evangelicals, and also to support the broader ecumenical discussion on Christian unity. In their eyes, by declining co-operation with fellow evangelicals Lloyd-Jones was introducing a division in evangelicalism where there was none before.

Lloyd-Jones replied that it was not he who had brought in the division; it was those who were introducing the policy of a double commitment. To allow the rightness of that policy would, in his judgment, be to produce such a change in evangelicalism that its historic meaning would be lost. Evangelicals should not, and could not, defend a unity with men who did not believe the same message. While he knew that those evangelicals who disagreed with him were not intending to undermine the gospel, he was convinced evangelicalism would not remain evangelicalism unless its practice was consistent with its belief. The uniqueness of the gospel message could not live with a policy of ecumenical openness, and he saw those who promoted that policy as the unwitting supporters of a situation in which what was distinctive about evangelical belief would be progressively weakened. As early as 1965, Lloyd-Jones was saying:

> We have evidence before our eyes that our staying amongst such people [i.e., non-evangelicals] does not seem to be converting them to our view but rather [is leading] to a lowering of the spiritual temperature of those who are staying amongst them and an increasing tendency to doctrinal accommodation and compromise.

What we have to assess here comes down to questions of historical fact. Has evangelicalism, since the 1960s, remained a movement of strong doctrinal convictions, asserting the supernatural over against the man-centredness and the expediency of so much contemporary religion? Has it kept to the fore what it means to be a Christian in contrast with the popular view which denies that, 'strait is the gate, and narrow is the way, which leadeth unto life, and few there be that find it'? I believe that on both sides of the Atlantic the evidence exists to prove that what Lloyd-Jones, Schaeffer and a few others feared has come to pass.

In England it can be seen, for instance, among many Anglican evangelicals who believed that 'openness' was the right policy in the 1960s. One of the leaders affirmed in 1973: 'Evangelicals recognize other Anglicans as fellow Christians, however critical they are of Evangelicalism.' Another leader went on record as saying that those who deny the virgin birth and the bodily resurrection of Christ do not 'forfeit the right to be called Christians'. In the case of a well-known bishop, who denied the resurrection of Christ, Anglican evangelicals now said that it was unworthy to entertain 'a lurking suspicion that this cannot be genuine Christianity'. In a book entitled *Anglican Evangelicals*, the two reputed evangelicals who wrote it asked for a contribution to its pages from the Bishop of Edinburgh, Richard Holloway, who was a liberal Anglo-Catholic. So Holloway wrote the final chapter in which he said that evangelical belief had no relevance to the question how anyone becomes a Christian; because, 'We are incorporated into Christ by baptism and grace.' He went on to write that it was inadmissible to make 'the substitutionary theory of the atonement one of the prime tests of doctrinal purity', and he deplored any practice which would make it a test of unity. Holloway's words were duly published without any expression of disagreement on the part of the editors. One of the men involved in the new evangelicalism within Anglicanism was George Carey. He is now the Archbishop of Canterbury, and his high office is sometimes adduced as proof of how evangelicals have now gained positions of leadership. But for Carey any exclusiveness for evangelical beliefs has long since gone. This is how he speaks about the Church of England:

> I remain convinced it is a broad Church combining the catholic, evangelical, charismatic and liberal in joyful harmony . . . For many of us in the Church, liberalism is a creative and constructive element for exploring theology today . . . It would constitute the end of Anglicanism as a significant force in world-wide Christianity if we lost this ingredient.

Yet such opinions did not prevent the Graham organization from inviting Archbishop Carey to speak at the congress in Amsterdam in 2000. The sad fact is that Graham himself has progressively lost any insistence on what makes an evangelical an evangelical. William Martin noted his 'diminishing dogmatism' and his 'ever-widening acceptance of others who professed to be Christians'. Graham says, 'The ecumenical movement has broadened my viewpoint.' Referring to differences between evangelicalism and Roman Catholicism he can say, 'I don't think the differences are important as far as personal salvation is concerned.' 'I feel I belong to all the churches. I am equally at home in an Anglican or Baptist or a Brethren assembly or a Roman Catholic church.'

In 1978 *McCall's* magazine quoted Graham as saying, 'I used to believe that pagans in far countries were lost if they did not have the gospel of Christ preached to them. I no longer believe that.' The Billy Graham Evangelistic Association and *Christianity Today* denied the authenticity of these words, but in 1997, on television for all to see and hear, Graham repeated the same statement in conversation with the liberal Dr Robert Schuller. The body of Christ, he told Schuller, would be made up

> from all the Christian groups around the world, outside the Christian groups. I think that everybody that loves or knows Christ, whether they are conscious of it or not, they are members of the body of Christ . . . they may not know the name of Jesus but they know in their hearts that they need something they do not have, and they turn to the only light they have, and I think that they are saved and going to be with us in heaven.

Schuller, with undisguised pleasure, cross-questioned the evangelist on the point: 'I hear you saying, that it's possible for Jesus Christ to come into human hearts and soul and life, even if they have been born in darkness and have never had exposure to the Bible. Is that the correct interpretation of what you are saying?' 'Yes, it is,' Graham responded in decided tones. At which Schuller exclaimed, 'I'm so thrilled to hear you say this.'

Why the Lloyd-Jones Understanding Differed

Lloyd-Jones died in 1981. It was a cause of great grief to him that precisely what he had warned against twenty years earlier was patently happening. Schaeffer felt the same. He wrote in 1984: 'What is the use of evangelicalism seeming to get larger and larger if sufficient numbers under the name evangelical no longer hold to that which makes evangelicalism evangelical?'

My point is that the evangelical 'openness', introduced and practised from the 1950s onwards, brought on a drift which its exponents never anticipated and have not been able to stop.[1] Few thought in the 1960s that thirty years later leading evangelicals would be calling the head of the Roman Catholic Church 'a wonderful Pope', or that a message from the pontiff would have been read at Graham meetings (as at Amsterdam in 2000), but it has happened.

Lloyd-Jones had no prophetic powers in anticipating what has happened but he had a good biblical reason for believing the future would develop as it has.

He knew that holding fast the purity of the faith, and our own assurance of it, is not something we can retain at will. We did not come to the faith by our own intelligence or by our own decision. It is by the illumination of the Holy Spirit that we believe what we do. It is not so much that Christians have come to hold convictions, but rather that convictions have laid hold on them. This means that where the Holy

[1] The conduct of Archbishop Leighton in the seventeenth century suggests a parallel with more recent leaders: 'Leighton's was one of many instances of a good man helping Christ's enemies out of apparent zeal for Christ, on grounds of theory that seemed to him quite sound, but miscalculating the necessary effect of his actions.' W. G. Blaikie, *The Preachers of Scotland* (reprint, Edinburgh: Banner of Truth, 2001), p. 146.

Spirit is grieved, convictions will weaken or even be lost. When the apostle says, 'Hold fast the form of sound words', he immediately adds, 'That good thing which was committed to you, keep [guard, watch] by the Holy Spirit who dwells in you' (*1 Tim.* 1:14). We are dependent on him. Horatius Bonar was a true reader of Scripture and of church history when he said, 'Fellowship between faith and unbelief must, sooner or later, be fatal to the former.' This is so, not because error is more powerful than truth, but because if we befriend the advocates of error, we will be deprived of the aid of the Spirit of truth. If we retain orthodoxy in word we shall certainly lose its power.

Wrong teaching about Christ and the gospel, according to Scripture, is deadly dangerous. Out of good motives we may seek to win influence for the gospel among those who are not its friends, but when we do so at the expense of truth, we shall not prosper in the sight of God. Eusebius, the early Christian historian, wrote:

> Such caution did the apostles and their disciples use, so as not even to have any communion, even in word, with any of those that thus mutilate the truth, according to the declaration of Paul: 'An heretical man after the first and second admonition avoid, know that such a one is perverse, and that he sins, bringing condemnation on himself.'

For Lloyd-Jones the most disturbing aspect of contemporary evangelicalism was the failure to depend upon God alone. He believed that if the necessity of the Spirit's power for the revival of the church had been put first, the toleration of the so-called openness would never have occurred. He feared the existence of an evangelicalism which sought influence by worldly thinking and worldly means. Connected with this worldliness, in his mind, was the small attention which evangelicals in general had come to give to the reality of the demonic. An ability to discern the demonic was no longer treated as a necessity. Thus, in the midst of apparent success, people could see no danger, and did not conceive of the possibility that the devil as an angel of light could himself have part in celebrating an evangelical renaissance.

As years passed, there was much which ought to have made evangelicals suspect their optimistic openness and recognize a deceiver at work in their midst. Consider these few quotations. James Davison Hunter, in his book, *Evangelicalism* (1987), wrote of evangelicals:

> There is less sharpness, less boldness, and, accordingly, a measure of opaqueness in their theological vision that did not exist in previous generations (at least to the present extent). A dynamic would appear to be operating that strikes at the very heart of Evangelical self-identity.

Commenting on the evangelical scene in the 1980s, Dr Carl Henry believed, 'Numerical bigness has become an infectious epidemic.'

Or again, Dr David Wells, referring to the appearance of evangelical strength, said, 'The perception was a mirage.'

If these assessments are not denied, whose influence ought they to suggest to us? An evangelical strategy which aimed at the best and yet, in important respects, turned out for the worst, was surely being affected by an influence other than that of God. Evangelicalism was too largely concentrating on numbers, on personalities, on publicity, on organization, when according to Scripture the real conflict is not in the realm of the visible at all. The main conflict is supernatural:

> We do not wrestle against flesh and blood, but against principalities, against powers, against the rulers of the darkness of this age, against spiritual hosts of wickedness in the heavenly places (*Eph*. 6:12).

The recognition of Satan is supremely important. It keeps before us the fact that evil is not merely an idea, it is a great and personal power. It teaches us that errors over the gospel are not innocent mistakes, they are demonic deceptions: there are counterfeit Christs and false gospels. The existence of Satan as the ruler of all unregenerate men and women is also a final proof that the difference between Christian and non-Christian is absolute and radical. We are not to please men, nor to fear men, says Scripture. Why not? For one reason, even if we please them and gain their approval, we gain nothing. 'Cease ye from man, whose breath is in his nostrils' (*Isa*. 2:22). No influence except that of God himself can meet the realities of their situation. That is the explanation of Paul's conduct at Corinth, 'And I, brethren, when I came to you, did not come with excellence of speech or of wisdom' (*1 Cor*. 2:1).

The Positive Alternative

From my references to Lloyd-Jones it would be a great mistake to conclude that his role was primarily a critical one. On the contrary, his main work was to present a positive alternative to the popular trend. He disputed the idea that evangelicals had to choose between ecumenical co-operation on the one hand and isolation. Another option was open and supremely needed, namely reliance on the power of the gospel. The churches in general were in the midst of a moral and social decay which they were powerless to alter. That fact did not dismay him for he knew that conditions equally deplorable had existed many times before.

In the early eighteenth century, materialism reigned, false charity prevailed, and conviction of sin had almost disappeared. The Wesleys and George Whitefield faced that situation by a direct and bold return to Scripture. Instead of seeking the support of fellow-churchmen, they were ready to stand alone, convinced it was by unfaithful preaching that the Church and the world had become mixed together. They made the recovery of the gospel and of what it means to be a Christian the one great need. Instead of making them popular this brought on intense opposition from the leaders of the Church of England. William Warburton, Bishop of Gloucester, demanded of John Wesley, 'Why do you talk of the success of the gospel in England, which was a Christian country before you were born?' To which Wesley replied:

> Was it indeed? Is it so at this day? – If men are not Christians till they are renewed after the image of Christ, and if the people of England, in general, are not so renewed, why do we term them so? 'The god of this world hath' long 'blinded their hearts'. Let us do nothing to increase their blindness; but rather recover them from that strong delusion, that they may no longer believe a lie.

After Wesley had preached at the University Church in Oxford on the subject, 'The Almost Christian', he was never allowed to speak there again. He demonstrated to his hearers on that occasion the marks of a real Christian, and then anticipated the objection which would be raised over the relevance to them of Paul's words to King Agrippa (*Acts* 26:28):

> 'O, but this is not a parallel case! For they were heathens; but I am a Christian.' A Christian! Are you so? Do you understand the word? Do you know what a Christian is? If you were a Christian you would have the mind of Christ; and you would walk as he also walked – Are you inwardly and outwardly holy? I fear, not even outwardly.

This was the issue which the evangelical leaders constantly pressed everywhere in the eighteenth-century awakening. They believed that the majority of the clergy fell under the same condemnation as the false prophets to whom God said, 'You have strengthened the hands of the wicked, so that he does not turn from his wicked way to save his life' (*Ezek*. 13:22). Their opponents said of them: 'Their doctrine is too strict; they make the way to heaven too narrow.' On which words Wesley made this all-important comment: 'And this is in truth the original objection (as it was almost the only one for some time), and is secretly at the bottom of a thousand more, which appear in various forms.'

In the same spirit Whitefield told the Bishop of London that he was treating nominal Christians as being in 'a very imperfect state', whereas the truth was that they were 'in no state of Christianity at all'.

The ministry of Dr Lloyd-Jones exemplified this same approach. He knew that the progress of the gospel today is not obstructed by new and unique problems which an adherence to Scripture cannot answer. The one great problem in every age is that the 'the natural man receives not the things of the Spirit of God'. The first need of men and women today is exactly the same as in the apostolic era or as in the days of Whitefield and Wesley: it is the need of regeneration. Human nature is engulfed in a spiritual deadness which nothing but the Spirit of God can remove. When that conviction prevails, then the question how opposition to evangelical truth is to be addressed takes on a very different answer:

> Put not your trust in princes, nor in the son of man, in whom there is no help. His breath goes forth, he returns to his earth; in that very day his thoughts perish. Happy is he that hath the God of Jacob for his help, whose hope is in the LORD his God (*Psa.* 146:3–5).

CONCLUSIONS

To judge situations chiefly by the appearance of things is always dangerous. Evangelical opinion in these last fifty years has been too largely influenced by what men believed they saw – numbers, attractive personalities, the charismatic 'revival', the friendliness of the new Roman Catholic policy, 'many Roman Catholics are true Christians', etc. But it is Scripture and not the observable that is the rule of faith. Our own hearts and our own understanding of events provide no trustworthy guide. 'Judge not according to the appearance, but judge righteous judgment' (*John* 7:24). 'There is a way which seems right unto a man, but the end thereof are the ways of death' (*Prov.* 14:12). The argument from apparent success or popularity is a particularly dangerous one. A religious majority generally uses such words as those with which Bunyan's 'Mr By-ends' describes the faithful:

> They are for holding their notions, though all other men be against them; but I am for religion in what, and so far as, the times and my safety will bear it. They are for religion when in rags and contempt; but I am for him when he walks in his silver slippers, in the sunshine, and with applause.

Our only security is real and continued communion with Christ. Correct belief is essential but it is not enough. We can be orthodox and yet proud, cold and careless. A thousand temptations surround us and, left to ourselves, any one of them would be enough to bring us down. Self-confidence is the greatest danger of all. 'Let him who thinks he stands take heed lest he falls' (*1 Cor.* 10:12). The only safe place to live, where we may have assurance of God's presence, is in 'the valley of humiliation,' where, Bunyan tells us, the shepherd's boy sang

He that is down, needs fear no fall;
He that is low, no pride;
He that is humble ever shall
Have God to be his guide.

> To this man will I look, even to him that is poor and of a contrite spirit, and trembles at my word (*Isa.* 66:1).

Reviewers' Comments on *Evangelicalism Divided:*

The book is a page turner from first to last . . . It left me asking, 'Has the last fifty years seen evangelicals broaden the road to the extent that the Christian message is compromised and uncertain?'

Peter Breckwoldt, *Church of England Newspaper*

Murray's critique is as kind as it is revealing and devastating. The icons of modern evangelism are shown as falling into egregious strategic errors which have weakened the evangelical faith at its very core. The bridges built to reach the mainstream became a two-way street by which those who sought to influence the liberals were themselves influenced.

R. C. Sproul, *Table Talk*

Names aren't important . . . What is important is assessing a bad strategy. Murray focuses on the strategy adopted by one American evangelistic organization and one segment of the Evangelical party in the Church of England. Both decided to get a wider hearing by making peace with nonevangelicals. The price of this peace was that evangelicals had to quit stressing their differences with Christianity's other branches. They had to concede that theirs was just one more outlook on the issues.

Mark R. Talbot, *Modern Reformation*

Evangelicalism Divided is a great book, and all who are concerned about the dilemma of evangelicalism – indeed the future of Christianity – will benefit greatly by familiarizing themselves with the information contained in it.

Larry Pettegrew, *Master's Seminary Journal*

Evangelicalism Divided is important reading for professed evangelicals who want to understand [evangelicalism's] recent history. It is not, of course, a history of evangelicalism.

Tom Wells, *Reformation Today*

Murray presents a convincing argument with cogent evidence. His ability to concentrate on the bigger picture, without ignoring necessary details, ensures that he takes the reader with him. There is no doubt that there will be readers of this book who will take exception to some of his conclusions, but the broad thesis stands firm. This book is probably one of the most important church history books published in 2000 and every church leader ought to read it.

BRIAN TALBOT, *SCOTTISH BAPTIST WEBSITE*

Iain Murray's startling analysis of the drift of modern evangelicalism is both informative and insightful. I share his concerns. I also appreciate his courage and his clarity. This is a much-needed word of exhortation to the church of our generation. It's one of the best and most eye-opening books I have read in years.

DR JOHN F. MACARTHUR

A vital warning, and British evangelicalism needs to take note.

JOHN BENTON, *EVANGELICALS NOW*

Far from being a merely academic work it is written with genuine pastoral concern. It ends with six conclusions:

- It is difficult to remedy a fault without running to the opposite extreme.
- Much of the confusion dividing evangelicals goes back to the question, 'Who is a Christian?'
- The Church cannot succeed as political parties do.
- Serious differences and controversies do arise among Christians.
- It is very hard for leaders to look in different directions at the same time.
- The struggles and hopes of Christians are not to be understood in present, temporal terms.

GRACE MAGAZINE